To My Ram

WITH LOVE

To My Ram

WITH LOVE

CHERYL KNOLL

Printed in the United States of America

ISBN 979-8-89114-145-2 (hc)
ISBN 979-8-89114-144-5 (sc)
ISBN 979-8-89114-146-9 (e)

Library of Congress Pre-assigned Control Number: 2024925509

2025.02.10

MainSpring Books
5901 W. Century Blvd
Suite 750
Los Angeles, CA, US, 90045

www.mainspringbooks.com

The Special Path

I looked back for a glimpse at the path
The path now paved with beautiful stones
Unseen by others, this one was mine
My destiny, the Lord God owns
Some stones were more beautiful than others
Those were the stones set in place with pain
Being unwanted and being rejected
Those were me suffering more loss than gain
God's words sealed them giving them shine
I looked at them noticing
They were all mine
They were laid in place some time ago
Suffering patience
Some were love that did not grow
At times, several laid in the same row
Though now they are polished and wear a glow

Those were tough times Lord
How did I get through
It was by your grace Lord
It was only you
You brought me to this place
Now I know who I am
You loved and blessed me
And you led me
To cross paths with my ram

Her Prayer

Though my life belongs to God
I was searching for my purpose and found a treasure
I prayed to God for this handsome ram
I love him with unmeasurable measure
Let this treasure be mine dear Lord
I find this treasure to be of great worth
He is a free and handsome strong ram
Not to be kept by anyone on earth

Dear Lord, who could keep me also but you
There are rare and special times two forces come together
Let this treasure be a gift I pray
You are the gift giver, and he is my pleasure

Please Lord, let me keep him I pray
I would hate to see my handsome ram get away

The Turbulence

I went through a storm in my heart
The storm left debris, obstacles in my way
Now I wear overcoming as my crown
As peace of mind and true love now stay
In a heart that was baron
Save for my love for God
I fell in love
Though love had no place to live
A whirlwind of pain and confusion was my storm
When I realized love found me
And I had love to give

Timing and patience may as well have been mountains
So huge, yet I overcame
All the while the turbulence of falling in love
My true love went through it the same
I will never forget the price of this journey
The price I paid to have him for my own
And God in His infinite wisdom and mercy
Gave me the greatest love ever known

Love's Path

I do not need others advice
I will find my own way
My destiny is calling me
To find true love to stay
I know where I am going
Though at times, took a wrong turn
To walk across the fiery trials
Feeling scorched
After a burn

Once I thought I found love
It seemed I could not make a dent
I felt as helpless as a flower
That grew to bloom in cracked cement
It was then I knew love could grow
Where I thought it could not live
And then I found the more love I gave
My recipient had love to give
He transplanted me into his fertile heart

His love was worth the wait
Divine timing has its own way
As does God
As does love and fate
I knew it was my own path
Others warned me not to take
When love calls, it outlives advice
When it finds love to make

Strong Enough to be Weak

My strong man makes me feel a bit weak
A little helpless as well
Now I will play the helpless damsel
My secret, please do not tell

He can hold me in his arms
Anytime he perceives I am weak
Softly I say "thank you handsome"
In my helpless voice I will speak

Me? I tire of being strong
And when he holds me to his chest
That is when I melt into his love
I am weak and give my strength a rest

When he holds me close to his heart
And he cannot see my face
I feel a little sneaky with my smile
And tonight
I will love him wearing lace

Telepathic Love

As the evening grows dark
I sit sipping my wine
My thoughts are of him
My ram is fine
Strong and handsome
His lips are full
We give and take
We push and pull
Is he out hunting wild game?
Wherever he is
He is mine just the same
My love for him will never end
Telepathically I will send
My love
I love you ram
I love you my ram
These are my words I send to you
From my heart and my mind
These sent words you will find
Will forever and ever be true

Flaming Sword

He had a flaming sword he brandished
Only I could see
His sword burned with fiery love
His love was meant for me
He swung his sword; his love cut deep
It left a flame of love to keep
So much love, the fire burns a flame
So much love, our two loves feel the same
So much love, it keeps me warm at night
So much love when his arms hold me tight
He has a flaming sword
Only I can see
His sword of flaming love
Hot love
His love only for me

Suffer the Fall

Falling in love
He was suffering
My strong man tried to fight
Love's fight
He was used to being his own man
Though love found him, and it was right
The feelings others search and seek
His were growing strong and he felt weak
Do not fight with love, it wins
It cannot stop once it begins
It strengthens you and makes you stronger
I cannot wait for you much longer
Listen to me as I speak
Love will make you strong, not weak

Love will always give you space
I just want to kiss your face
And hug you and lay by your side
Embrace this love you cannot hide
You will be okay tonight
Suffer the fall and hold me tight
The love I give you should not fight
You cannot fight true love
Listen my love, as I speak
Love will make you strong
Not weak

Love Is

Love is ever searching
Love is ever seeking
Love is not containable
Love is softly speaking
Growing, spreading, ever rising
When love finds new hearts
It fills with surprising
When newly found
Some hearts grow to burst
The best love is unconditional
Love gives forgiveness first
The hardest hearts soften
Anxiety stills
Love enters unloved hearts
And overfills
Love brings life
To all that it finds
The most wonderful love
Is in hearts
Love binds

One Set of Footsteps

One set of footsteps
Walking through fall leaves
Wish for another set of footsteps
Yours
My footsteps are wishing for yours
My hands are reaching
For your arm to hold
My eyes are looking to see yours
Looking at me
The silence in my ears listen
To hear your voice speak to me
Let's walk through the trees
Walking on the leaves
To share love
In Autumn
In love

Time Stands Still

I could not bear any added hours to the day
Time stands still
When the one I love is away
I wake in the morning
And wait for the night to return
Every hour feels like a fire that is fed
But will not burn
I wait to sleep in another dimension
Where missing you does not bring more pain
Until I am united with the one, I love
I feel as though I am bound in chain
Bring our two hearts and bodies together
Reunite our hands, our lips, our arms
Reunite these two flames that burn for one another
Where separation no longer harms
Then I can live through all the days hours
When the one I love will share those hours with me
Love will erase all our missing hours
And time will fly again
Love is timeless
Love sets time free

Love's Light Calls

The light called my name
I answered the call
I knew the light that called
Afterall
It reminded me of whence I came
Even when I wander
We know each other the same
The light has spoken to my heart
Of you
The light is never wrong
It shined upon the path to take
And to you, I would belong
We will belong to each other
Something our hearts always knew
Two flames who belong together
A fiery love
Between me and you
The light gives bits
Of glorious brightness
To shine on hearts
To hold with hands
Love more valuable than gold
Sometimes it does not call
It demands

The Ram She Loves

The northern country
Calls for the ram I love
He, all masculine
Journeys to his majestic stay
He has traveled away
Behind is the heart that beats for him
A heart that is full of love for her ram
She knows his ways
She is full of joy for him
She will wait for the day of his return
He will have his way with her
And she with him
For he is the ram she loves
When the water shines like glass
And his ways are eased
He will be pleased
To go home

He Makes Me Shine

The branches and twigs sparkled in the night
Glitter made of sleet that shone in the light
I look out a dark window though I am all right
Just alone
Missing the man that is only my own
When the light goes out and the glitter does not shine
In the light
The sleet that once sparkled is now just water
In the night
That is how missing feels
And tears want to fall, and they might
I am just missing the man
Whose light shines
And brings glitter to my night

Sanctified Love

It was love that sanctified their path
They gave their love but never wrath
Their love was warm
It shined like light
They held on to each other tight
A blessing so few people find
To live their love so deep and kind
Respecting differences they found
Forgiveness was their solid ground
They would look into each other's eyes
Often seeing a surprise
It was their love they shared
A reflective gleam
It was true love
They lived their dream

When it Rains

When it rains and we are apart
We are not
You are here in my heart
And in my mind, I see you here
And in my bed, I feel you near
When the rain is softly falling
I look forward to you calling
You will say "come stay with me"
And we will make love, and it will be
Like the rain
When it rains
Like the wind and the rain
We will make love and make love again
When it rains
With fierce winds
We make love like a storm
Then it eases and our love is gentle and warm
You tell me you want me here in your bed
In person to hold
Not just in your head
Now I am here, and I love you
And you love me too
And it is raining my love
And we know what to do
When it rains

Spoken Fire

There is a voice of fire in my heart
Let it burn as a sacred flame
Let us both keep this torch burning
This fire grows when you say my name
That is my proof that this flame is God given
The sound of your voice when you say my name
Every time I hear it, it goes to my heart
Tell me when I speak
You feel the same

Trees and Love

I stood on the ground next to the trees
Looking to the sky
Reverence filled my heart so full
All I could do was sigh
When I saw how high they reached
How much closer to God were these
Suddenly I felt as though I were nothing
Just nothing that no one sees
But reason returned and I was whole
I know God, he keeps my soul
My heart, my soul, my mind
I would find
Gave reverence to God
Who created the trees
Could anything move my heart
Like these?
Only love Lord, only love
Dear Lord, I know I found the man
Can any man on this earth move my heart
Yes Lord, I found this man can

He Has My Attention

When I am alone with him
The world's clutter goes away
My mind frees itself of what others have done
Or what they had to say
My mind focuses on his thoughts
And everything he has said
His opinions interest me
I love that brain inside his head
My mind is calmed with his stability
As I have a mind that runs wild and free
It runs with God and angels and fate
Flames of love and manifesting desires
Without wait
I have an imagination creating life inside my mind
But also, passion, compassion, and love
So deep and kind
Only one man can free my mind
From its wanderings and its games
It is him, they are his words
That ground me with love that tames
His mind reasons with logic
That is why I love what goes on in his head
Though I will balance that
With my mind running free
And wild
When we are in bed

Autumn Date

Love is burning Autumn colors in my heart
To be in love in the fall
To be in love with him, with leaves falling
To be in the house where it is warm inside
My phone is ringing, he is calling
It will be a good night to snuggle later
After he takes me out for our date
I do not care that it is chilly outside
I want to see him
I cannot wait
He will have a blush of pink on his cheeks
He is so handsome in the colors of fall
I will warm his cheeks
As I hold his face and kiss him
To show appreciation for his call

From Me to You

What I felt was not a game
I love my man
I love his name
I love his lips
His strong arms too
For me, no other man will do
I once felt love had passed me by
I prayed to God and wondered why
Living loveless, unaware
God found a man with love to share
Not every pair can love this way
Deeply in love everyday
This is rare love
Meant to feel
It comes from God and lives as real

God gave me what I rightfully deserved
He kept a wonderful man reserved
In God's timing I patiently waited
For my true love that God had fated
God is great and always good
To bring me love
As only He could

When Love Meets

Secret feelings can hide in hearts
Though when these two hearts are near
One another
Love is breathed into the secret
No longer will love be hidden
These two hearts know each other
And in love's own ways
These two hearts reach for one another
With a silent touch
The silence, then overpowered
By an internal pounding
Desire has spoken to love
Secret no more

Force Meets Force

No force can control my ram
He is free
Though forces meet forces
The force he met was me
My love is a force
It rages and it is strong
It was searching for a force
Where it would belong
My ram needs his space
Where he can live and be free
My unconditional love, ram
My force, I give to thee
Ram, when you tire
Come home to me
My force is love
I will show you
You will see

His Outline

I saw the outline of his body
Within that, his universe to see
A galaxy of love and fire
This man was saving his love for me

God gives the greatest love ever known
Now he gifted me with a man of my own
I will keep his love and tend it
As a fire
Loving a twin flame
Your love ascends higher

His love is shining and
I see my reflection
I thanked God for leading this man
My direction
Just when you have given up on love
It appears
When you
Think God does not hear your prayers
He hears
When you see your world in the outline of a man
Is it possible to see this?
Yes
With God you can

Gift of Touch

He does not have to buy gifts for me
The gift I love is feeling his touch
I am in heaven being in his arms
And holding his hand, just as much
I love him putting his hands on my shoulders
Even more, his hand resting on my thigh
I never ask him; it is part of his love for me
He loves me and loves touch does not lie
Love can connect with touch conversation
I do not have to speak words for a reply
I can just squeeze his hand when he touches me
Or wink to see love's touch in his eye

The Illness

This illness did not serve him well
His mind was dull, he felt like hell
At work he could not concentrate
He did not enjoy what he ate
At night he could not fall asleep
He was in love
He was in deep
He wondered how he would get by
There were rare times he wanted to cry
He was lovesick that is for sure
She would be his only cure

At times she hoped he was crying
Inside she felt like she was dying
She hoped he was suffering too
For her, no other man would do
She was lovesick, feeling blue
She had the illness
She loved him too

You Chose Me

The care he gives me, I return with respect
Never in my life would I bring him down
I will uplift him with unconditional love
If he disappointed me, I would not show the slightest frown

Every day, I will tell him I love him
Not only will I say it
He will feel it too
I will tell everyone how much I love him
For me, no other man will do
Honey, I love you and
I will strive to be the best I can be
And reflect with respect
The love and care you give
You were not looking for a woman
But you chose me

The Painful Awakening

I looked out into the night for so many years
Wondering what I was missing
Wondering what these feelings were
As if something I was dismissing
These feelings ate at my heart and soul
Feelings I could not control
I did not know what there was to find
Then I met you and you lived in my mind

I wondered about this painful game
In my head you were mine
My own twin flame
My mind went crazy, it was not free
You had a power over me
Every waking moment was pain
I wondered if I was even sane
And the love that overwhelmed me to tears
It was you I was missing for so many years
It was you who my heart and body ached for
It was you I wanted, and I wanted you more

It was pain so deep and real I could die
At times, all I could do was cry
God made my soul aware and rescued me
He stilled my mind and set me free
I found the love that I could give
I loved myself first
Now love can live
I can live again, and the pain has died
Not me
Those painful times are now a distant memory

The price I paid was suffering
And I know I will never be the same
A great price was paid for the greatest love
The love I receive from my twin flame

He Painted Me with Love

My heart had become an empty canvas
I had forgotten how love could feel
Then he came into my life
With colors of his love to heal
With gentle strokes and skillful eyes
He captured me to my surprise
He painted me with his healing love
With feelings no other man could capture
He stroked me with his words of love
We both transformed in loving rapture
With brushstrokes of love, he completed me
He made sure his love had filled my heart
His colors spilled into my soul
To never fade or ever part
He gave me sight and gave me a vision
Where once my heart was empty and bare
Though my heart held the love of God
There was no man's love in there

I am his now; he is mine
His love is mine with a grateful heart
I never knew what true love was
His love more beautiful than art
He transformed my empty heart
With the deepest love that would not fade
I felt his love as he held me close
The love kept painting as we laid
I am his now; he is mine
I belong to the artist whose love could see
He painted me with love, his love
Brushstrokes of his love for me

Chosen Ram

He is my chosen ram
He is my handsome ram
He is strong
His masculinity he wears as horns
He will push the weak aside
As he searches for me
And he will find me
I will stand waiting for him
Our encounter, a force of nature
A predestined gift from God Almighty
It is God who created mating
God's plans from the foundation
I stand on His earth in reverence
God chose us to share love
God has chosen this love for me
My chosen ram

Nighttime Reflections

In the quiet of the night
My heart is neither quiet nor still
It beats for the love of my life
I know it always will
The busy tasks of the day
Can barely fill my thoughts
I think of us laying in our bare skin
My mind ends up in knots
He is my one true earthly love
His love is my greatest earthly treasure
There is no way to weigh my love for him
No earthly way to measure

Ask for Love

I asked the universe to give
To me
True love that would live
And be
The reason that I breathe and live
God's universe has love to give
The love I get
I will return
The more I love
The more I learn
The love God's universe will give
It should be shared
For love to live

All I Need

All that is material does not entice
Having less to me is nice
What I live for
My desire
You and me
In love
Hearts on fire

Soul Light

The sun peeks into the dark sky
Dawn embraces the sun
Their interaction awakens another day of light
I meditated on their engagement
His soul awakened a new light in my soul
What did you do to me?
Peeking and shining your light
Light met light
An engaging happened
Illuminating the light that is love
His light awakened love
When love awakens
It is unstoppable
It will shine

Without Your Love

Green leaves would turn to blue
If my life did not include you

The sun would only shine with brown
My smile would turn into a frown

All my flowers would bloom dull gray
They would only bloom one day
Just one bloom and they would die
As would I
As would I

If I did not have you nearby
My world would be without the sky
Just dirt and ground
Music with no sound

Without your love
That is how I would feel
I am grateful you are mine
And
Your love for me is real

Memory Photo

When I look at you
And our eyes meet
I see the smile in your eyes
At times, your eyes glisten with love
These are the times I take a memory photo
I keep these beautiful moments in my mind
I keep copies in my heart as well
These memories of you are my treasure
I am wealthy in love
Your love

I See Love

I see him with more than my eyes
Vision that emanates from my heart
Unconditional love that covers all wrongs
I see it even when we are apart

I feel him with more than my body
I feel him with my heart and soul
With a mystical touch that cannot be felt
When we are separated, I still feel whole

And when I see him through my own eyes
And I feel him with my body and hands
With my heart and soul and my love out of control
All my senses desire his commands

A Perfect Day

I woke this morning, the ground was white
My lover was nowhere in sight
The tracks of wild game now show
The wilderness called him
He had to go

No hurry to get out of bed
The love we made still fills my head
A luxurious bath, then I will bake
And frost and eat some chocolate cake
I will exercise until I tire
Then bathe again and watch the fire
My heart flutters when he returns
There is more than one kind of fire that burns

The Invitation

The ram moves through the flowers
He knows his way
He has a destination
His inner compass guides him
He knows her ways also
She has been waiting for him
She sends an invitation
Does he stop and smell the flowers?
Not really, he is not smelling the flowers
He has an invitation
And nothing can distract him
He is my ram

Hi Handsome

I love my rugged outdoors man
The wilderness has him looking handsome
His untamed beard
His pink blushed cheeks
His full lips slightly blue
When cold and numb
Lord, he has me under his thumb
And even though I am free
Under his spell I love to be
I love my man
He is all man
His masculinity, his consternation
When our bodies touch
We have conversation
All the "she" in me
Is grateful he
Is my rugged outdoors man
And all my "she"
Gives him all my love
Every chance I can

Love Yourself

When love does not live anymore
Where does it go when it dies?
When it once burned strong and flamed
Now its memories only bring sighs
The only answer I find
This love may not have been real
The only way to live again
Is love yourself
You will heal

Reciprocating Love

What can I give to you
In return for your love
I will give you the best version of myself
I will give you all that I have
My words of love are only for you
I will give you all the space you need
My love will not be a clinging love
Unless we are making love
Then I will cling to your love
Then I will cling
In that clinging
All the love you have given to me
Will be reciprocated
All my love
Is for you

Love Awakens

Love is ever seeking
I was as a tree in the dark of night
Just being, though not seen
Then love, like the moonlight appeared
It illuminated what was hidden
Love shone on me and softly whispered
You are beautiful in the darkness
It is time to let your beauty shine in love
The moonlight also whispered
As it touched me
See now, a grand light will shine
I came to awaken love in you
It is a powerful love
You will be seen now
In the light of love

Telepathic Invitation

On a quiet morning with an overcast sky
I miss my ram though no need to cry
A gentle breeze moving leaves on the trees
My heart sends an invitation
Come over and visit me please
The sun's scorch is absent today
Also absent, my ram
He is off to play
He is enjoying his masculine endeavors
I also wish to enjoy my own endeavors
With his masculinity

On this "missing you" morning
Where are you, my ram?
I feel desperate to call your phone
Just to hear your voice say "yes ma'am"
Please surprise me and make my day
You know we both love cloudy morning play
Right now,
I would love to feel your arms
Where are you, my ram?
Stop by
I am out of the shower
Wearing summer tanned skin
What I would not give
To see your wink and your grin

I Choose You

We are co-creators of our own destiny
I choose you to be my own
I choose you to hold me close
To be the greatest love I have ever known
The love I feel, transcends boundaries
I will cross boundaries to be with you
I will cross rivers or mountains
Or realities
Anything in my way I will get through

Unconditional love is my vessel
It will get me through anything in my way
If co-creating comes with a cost
There is no amount I will not pay
I choose you in my created reality
I choose you to have me for your own
I have love to give to you and you only
It will be the greatest love
We have ever known

Till You Return

Sunny summer days now wane
My longing for you blossoms pain
My mind tries to make you real
Your body, how it makes me feel
I miss you
You will help me heal
When we kiss
My lips, your lips seal
I am yours till you return
Till then
A different sun will shine and burn

Alas, the blooming flowers fade
My days of missing you will end
I still feel you standing near me
All my love to you I send
Keep my love and think of me
I long for the day when you I see
The sun for me will once more shine
When you hold me
When you are here
And mine

The Shadow's Secret

I turned and looked to the west
I saw the shadow's darkness
A secret in that darkness
As I looked away
I turned and looked again
My soul beckoned to his, come out
He was there
I saw his vulnerability
I knew I loved him
He had every strength a man should have
Even in his vulnerability
He was strong
When we looked at each other
Unconditional love filled my heart
My heart found where it belonged
It was his
Not a secret
To hide in the shadows

Recycling

I see the leaves as they turn gold
Like people, leaves, they too grow old
Their grip grows weak
They let go
They drift or fall to ground below
As we grow old
We too let go
The once high minded
Now lay low
The youthful strength
No more to show
We all return to the earth below our feet
What made it all worthwhile
Your love, so sweet
I pray our love, our souls
Again, will meet

My Fortress of Love

You are a fortress of love for me
You have a strength that cannot be diminished
You brought an awakening to my soul
Though I was ever aware of my soul
You awakened it in my body
Now it lives as never before
You awoke an awareness in me
You brought me to the place
Where I could still my mind
The mind's games and stories quelled
Peace of mind, a blissful gift
Love is a gift
Love is a gift giver
How can I repay you for your love
Except to give you my love and myself
I found my place in your fortress of love
I will not stray
In your fortress I will stay

Love Glows

Love births new light
As a candle lit in the darkness
Just as seeing my vision in a mirror
And being surprised
I look more radiant with love
The vision of myself
Seeing love that shows
Like a candle in the darkness
The light that burns
Glows

I am Here Smiling

The ram roams about
In his restless ways
I have not seen him
For many days
Does he think of me?
As I think of him
Chances are his thoughts are slim
Or
Is he replenishing his testosterone?
And when it is bursting
I will be his own
Send a message dear ram
Send a message to me
I am torn up inside
When you are nowhere to see
Though know in your heart
I love you to be free
Know also I am yours
And you belong to me

Crazy (In Love)

Today, my first day my mind felt relief
For months you have lived in my mind
To what do I owe this outstanding pleasure
To be free of you, yet I find
I hope this feeling passes also
And you again take up residence
Either way you drive me crazy
Crazy in love; does that make sense?

Communicating

He is vocal and I love to hear his voice
My words are fewer, and writing is my choice
Only
When we are alone
I always have words to say
I will tell him that I thought of him
All throughout the day
I will tell him I missed him
And I was waiting for us to kiss
I will tell him that I love his hugs
I will say all of this
Then later
When it is time for bed
I will give my words a rest
I will show him how I really feel
That is how I express myself the best

Welcome Home

Honey, please kiss me now that you are home
You can hug me while you are kissing me
You can say my name while we are hugging and kissing
We can make love because I have been missing you

Honey, welcome home
Now I have plans for you
Now I have things for you to do

The lightbulb in the bathroom is out and needs changing
A few pieces of furniture need re-arranging
The trash is full and needs to go out
Get them done quickly before I pout

Honey, I am just teasing
These chores are all done
I bought something see through
I want you to have fun
I need hugging and kissing
And your love I have been missing
When you roam
Let me show you how much I missed you
Welcome home

The Hidden Tears

If my heart could hold any more love for him
It would spill out in the form of tears
It is an emotional love in a sacred space
His love protects me from doubts and fears

I asked "dear Lord, how can this love be real?
When for so many years I had nothing to feel
I was your vessel for your love and for praying
Though when I awoke to his love it was staying"

I never knew these feelings in the empty years
Now the force of his love can bring me to tears
Grateful and deserving and worthy you saw me
You removed the empty years and set me free
Free to accept love from a man
Who gives it so extraordinarily as only he can
The greatest love that I could ever hope to be mine
Lord for now, I will hide my tears
Love's hidden tears shine

Rose Petals

Heavy snow starts falling
Excited birds are flying
The wind began blowing
But my heart is not sighing
We can set the rose petals on fire
We can lay on them
While satisfying our desire
I have my eyes on you
What I am manifesting is real
It is not the rose petals I wish to feel
I scattered them on the bed nonetheless
The fragrance will enhance the feel of your caress
Love making will not be only for me
I have something special for you
You will see
My wanting you is becoming dire
I love you, now let us
Set the rose petals on fire

Love Tug of War

It felt like a spiritual tug of war
The pulling was shifting, raising the bar
There was giving and taking
Both wanted love making
And they did, with these two
There was no forsaking
He was divinely masculine
Independance of his own
She was divinely feminine
Her love, mature and full grown
He would give, though not enough to take
Her love came freely
She was patient for his love's sake
This love was going to live and give
Occasionally tug of wars are stalemated
They would both be winners here
This tug of war
True love was fated

The Candle Burns

I will keep a candle burning for you
To remind me of the flame in my heart
To remind me of the warmth of your hugs
To shine your way back when we are apart
When it flickers it will remind me of laughter
Recalling your humor makes me smile
Forever and all time when you need me
I will carry this candle the extra mile

This candle of mine keeps my thoughts of you
I will keep this candle flame burning
I will tend it and keep it safe
As I wait for your returning
When you are home and mine once more
I will put the flame out on this candle
A new fire will ignite in my heart
When you are here, in person to handle
Lover, I have been waiting for you
Now we can let our own passion flame
Our fires are calling for a union
I have fire that I need you to tame

More than a Touch

It was a simple gesture of holding my hand
Though my heart wanted me to understand
Love can awaken with just a touch
When skin touches skin. I knew as much
I wanted more than the touch of his hand on mine
I wanted to kiss his neck
It smelled of sandalwood and pine
I wanted to feel his bare skin of his arms around me
I wanted to be in his bed at night with dimmed lights to see
His hands, his arms, his heart
And hear his voice
Having all of him would be my choice
I wanted to have him in every way
In every way and every day
And every night with his lips to kiss
Him holding my hand could lead to this
For now, I will savor the touch of his skin
I look forward to when the other touching will begin

Sacred Seal

Heaven put a sacred seal on our love
It is the rarest love
I have ever known
It is love that comes from the utter depth
In my deepest heart and soul
God has given me your love for my own
A sacred seal that we will never love another
Love blessed by God
With angels guiding
There is only one man who was created for me
You are mine
With you, I will be abiding

Light and Shadow

He is my light, and I am his shadow
I will follow him anywhere he will go
At times we transform, and I am the light
Anytime I want my love for him to show

I feel safe when he is my shadow
Always keeping me safe from behind
We transform in love, and he is my light again
Transforming is beautiful in love intertwined

I feel the light of love in his shadow
He lights my heart and wherever he stands
I am in the love shadow that he cast
I am the one there
In love at last

Strong Man

Though he is strong, he loves me tenderly
Though he is strong, he is tender holding me
His love is soft within his strength
And he will go to any length
To bestow on me his tender side
It is only with me his softness he does not hide
In his strength his tender love can show
In his tenderness, I see his strength glow
All my love is for you, my sweet strong man
Give me your tender love
As only a strong man can

Love Above All

My dear lover
You are a rare gift
A ship's cargo has no value
Compared to your love
Sunken treasures of the sea
Can lay
Trains filled with valuable freight
Can pass by me
No, none of these are for me
The love you bestow to me
More valuable than wealth
Gold can sit heavy
Silver can tarnish
I will value your love
Above all

Strolling With Angels

I stroll through the forest
Angels by my sides
As if holding my hands
No fear I will feel
The trees in their darkness
Will now see my light
They will glow with new beauty
Their darkness, now bright
Now in the brightness
There you stood in rare form
The closer I came to you
I could feel your love, warm
The angels were leading me
To a destiny planned
Fate sealed their mission
When you took my hand

Winks and Whispers

Winks and whispers
If not whispers
Words
In a low soft voice
Occasional soft touches
Sometimes firm
Oh, the firm ones that turn
Into an embrace
Where his hands move on my skin
When they stay in the right place
Then I look up
And our lips touch
We engage in a soft kiss
Then everything in this world goes away
Now, our entire world is this

Feisty Ram

Today is a bit drizzly, foggy, and gray
My ram, a bit feisty
He went away
He was in a mood
That did not suit me
He was disrespectful
So, I set him free
I opened the door with love
And let him go
That is what tough love is all about
You know
I love him more than the day before
And he will return, and I will love him even more
My ram needs his space
To reflect on his ways
He will change his attitude
In one or more days
He will see he was wrong and
His improved sight
He will feel loving
And come back and hold me tight
Feisty rams turn into lover rams at night

Game Over

I know we are divine counterparts
I belong to him, and he belongs to me
Though, how does the chaser make the runner
Realize and see
You cannot move on from your own soul
He is the part of me that makes me whole
One will chase and the other will run
This part of the journey is troubling
Not fun
After some time in this game so strange
Roles again, may change and exchange
It is a fragile move to bring about union
To be together in love making love communion
It is time for divine counterparts
To stop and join flames
And stop these tiring running and chasing games

Love is My Dessert

I can set my desire for sweets aside
Desserts I do not crave
Compared to true love
Love so sweet
Also, kind, and deep
My true love can touch me
Even as I sleep
When I awake
I am in awe of what I feel
To connect with true love
In a dream
Or
In another dimension
So real
When love leaves my heart full
When love fills my mind with ease
There are no sweet confections
That can compare to these

Slaying Dragons

Overcoming the separation
Of love calling to unite
With a sword to slay dragons
A spiritual fight
The dark night of the soul
No, not one mere night
But time that seems endless
With no end in sight
Fighting beasts, trying to stop our love
On its way
Go ahead
Send more dragons to slay
I will mortally wound them
I have God, I will pray
To help with these battles
To let love find its way

My soul will battle obstacles
Or fight many fights
To let true love's flames join
To be the brightest of lights
Be it dragons or darkness
Separation or lonely pain
With a sword that burns with fire
With flames that fall as rain
I will use the power of love
Any dragon I will slay
To unite our love
We belong together
I am a dragon slayer
Dead, they will lay

Sharing Love Words

He said "I love you" as the snow began to fall
Those words touched her heart
She treasured them all
She felt loved and cherished as only a woman could
She loved her man completely and she always would
"I love you too" she said as the snow fell at night
He leaned in to kiss her
To his side he squeezed her tight
Their love was beautiful like the falling snow
It covers imperfections and has a special glow
She loved his strong arms and spoke
"Please do not let go"
The love they shared, no measurement could know
God blessed this love
Between this woman and this man
Two hearts full of love
Who could do this?
God can

Wildfire, Wildflower

His love burned like a wildfire
Igniting, burning out of control
Her love burned like a wildflower
Wild and natural, reflecting her soul
When these two unite in love
There is no turning back
When these two give each other love
They know there is no lack

Firey flowers and flowery fires
Both burning passionately with desires
Flames of love unite and rage
Into fires of love that transcend age
At times when the embers smolder low
They breeze by each other
And sparks will grow into flames
And playfully they will entertain
Their fiery and flowery games

He is All Man

In his glorious masculinity she glows
As a flame in the night, he radiates
Evoking desire and passion in her femininity
He can flare his masculine flame
She can match it and tame it with her love
She will embrace the flame
With open arms she reaches for his embrace
Inseparable, the union
A love so strong the fire cannot be quelled
Nor should it be
A fire must be fed
She will feed the fire

Just Sitting

At times
Love can shine in stillness
When we sit together
And do not touch
I take comfort in sitting in his presence
Absorbing his strength
Love speaks in such times
I feel his love just being near him
An occasional wink speaks volumes
To my heart
It means he is feeling my love
For him also
Even when we sit apart

Destiny Leads

I felt the hands of destiny
Guiding me along its way
I did not know where I was going
At times I had no say
Yet destiny was ever knowing
The universe its guiding force
I just stayed to the hidden guiding
Knowing I must stay its course
Often, I felt DeJa'Vu
As if I once knew this place
Destiny delivered me
I knew this once I saw his face

I knew the moment I first saw him
It was not instant love but something rare
It was a magnetic attraction
My heart knew there was something there
It was not love I was seeking
Though destiny gave love control
I love this man and will forever
Now that we share one heart and one soul

I Love Him

The sky wears heaviness, ready to fall
Oh, dear Lord, I am missing my ram
Snow begins falling heavy and slow
I love him like the falling snow
It covers him, his heart I know
I blanket him with unconditional love
Like snow from the heavy sky above
My love for him is pure and deep
All my love is his to keep
Dear ram you know I am missing you
I love you
No other man will do
No, snow cannot stop my ram from getting through
I know my ram, he loves me too

Love Grows

Love can seep into any crevice
Of any heart not seeking love to find
It roots in secret
Love starts growing slowly
Expanding to the soul and mind
The heart gives life
To love unexpected
It nourishes love
It keeps it protected
Love grows in size
And shines through the eyes
When these eyes see
The one this love detected

Angel Messages

Though she walks alone, she takes it in stride
She walks with angels by her side
Worldly words and ways are left
To worldly minds with truth bereft
Her angels guide her and love her with care
With an abundance of angel messages, they share
They show their numbers when one awakes
Synchronicities
For the awakened one's sakes
Every message, she feels joy inside
She is grateful, she lets her angels guide
She did not know what she was looking for
One look into each other's eyes
It grew to be more
Unexpectedly, love was found
Now to this new path,
She must stay bound
Her angels tell her she is well on her way
The man she loves will be hers one day
They showed her a vessel
It grew to be huge in size
It was full of his love for her
No surprise
Now with loving messages
The angels guide her way
The love between these two
Was destined
And will stay

As I Waited

I looked up to the sky
I was looking for you
I looked to the trees
Waiting for you to walk out
I looked to the ocean
Waiting for you
To sail to the shore
I looked to the ground
Waiting to see your feet
In front of mine
All I wanted to see
Was you in front of me
You will be worth the wait
The pain of waiting will disappear
When you are mine
God's timing is divine
God and my angels comforted me
As I waited

I wait for him
Ready to be held
In his comforting tight embrace
I was created to be held in his arms
Blessed that his strong arms
Come with a handsome face
And a smart mind that told him
He wants me
His own way of loving me
Worthy of the wait

Snow Play

When the snow is coming down
And your arms are holding me
We are safe and warm inside
In your arms is where I love to be
I love it when you hold me close
The snow is falling, growing deep
I think we should go to bed
Though it is much too early to sleep
Your arms are the only arms for me
You have magic love that makes my day
I mentioned it is too early to sleep
I am wondering if you want to play?
Later, after I have had my way
You will hold me after loving play
It could snow deep every day
When you hold me in your arms that way

The Sweet Kiss

Thank you for the kiss
I felt it, soft and sweet
I felt you last night and it was real
In a dream, I felt your heat
You let me slide beneath you
I felt safe and warm
You said you only wanted me
Like it was real, in real form

It is amazing how real things seem
So real, we were together in a dream

No Rejecting This Love

If you would reject the gift of my love
I may suffer death without dying
My heart would suffer a sorrowful pain
It would exceed the emotion of crying
Rejection can be as death in love's game
Rejection and death can dress the same
Like grief, receiving a bouquet of white flowers
To turn brown and dry
As you stare for hours
No rejection will our love see
I love you and you love me
Our love is magnetized
It cannot suffer rejection
We will always have love and
Only loves reflection

The Reunion

In his absence
Waiting and hope become a union
Walking side by side
When would his presence and hers
Once more abide
Alas the day
She trembled at his sight
Hold me lover
Hold me my love, this very night
I can faintly stand in your presence
If your arms could hold me
They would remedy my state
Lover, if your lips softly
Touch my lips
I fear I should faint
Though kiss me lover
And let fate take its course
Kiss me lover. I missed your masculine force

The Force of Love

The force of nature cannot be controlled
Nothing can stop it
It must be
Love can be a greater force
Stronger than nature
Between you and me

How can you reckon with a force?
But to give in and let it have its way
The force of love seeks and searches
It may blow through
Or it will stay

Love is a force
From the greatest source
It must happen
Let it be
Love is a force
From God our source
It had to happen between you and me

One Now

You are not only my lover
You are my life, you are my living
You are the blood that flows through my heart
You are my arms opened wide for giving
You are my oxygen that keeps me breathing
You are my thoughts expanding and knowing
You are my heart so full of love
My love for you, just keeps growing
When two become one
There is only one body
Only one heart
Only one soul
Only one life now
Only life to its fullest
And whenever we make love
Our body is whole

Separation to Surrender

I surrender my love to you
My offering to you, it is all yours
You are the only recipient
I will prove it tonight behind closed doors

Separation cannot stifle my love
While you are away, my love keeps growing
I nurture and protect it and keep it safe
Now that I see you my love is overflowing

I surrender my heart and love to you
I lived on heartstrings to make it through
Separation was painful, now what will we do?
After making love for an hour or two

We may make more love for something to do

I could kiss your lips till they become sore
And we would both love that
And we would want more
I hope no one calls or knocks on the door

I will be surrendering my love to you

The Fix

Lord, can you restore my heart?
It is a mess of sorts
I cannot find me
My heart is missing something, Lord
Something only, you can see

My carefree days have shifted away
To missing the love, I want everyday
I know a doctor cannot fix my heart
Only you
Can find the missing part

Now Lord, that part is around six feet tall
He is handsome and smart
And after all
You want me to have the desires of my heart
I know it is him
The missing part

I know that man can make my heart well
I want his love to fill every cell
I know patience is a virtue
But virtue can be hell
It is your timing Lord, and
Hurry, make it tell

Love, My Favorite Season

Summer is passing into Autumn
The changing seasons touch my soul
I see the first glimpse of colors morphing
As another summer has taken its toll
And like summer to fall
Change comes to all
The change sends my ram traveling
To higher lands
I will miss the touch of his hands

Seasons change and I understand his ways
When the sky is gray, and I see the sun's rays

I will think of him and send him my love
Go handsome ram and please return
While you are absent
My passion will burn
Only the seasons will change with me
Not my love
I am saving it all for you
You will see

I Found It

Let the summer wine be sweet
Let memories of me be good
I let love in to fill my heart
I honored God as we all should
The days I live may not seem many
Though I will live forever more
I sought the truth
I found the love
The key to God's eternal door
When I leave this realm behind
I will wait for you
I will save your place
Grateful for the love you gave me
And the best lips and kisses
And your handsome face

Blue Jay Blue

Birch branches bearing golden leaves
Changing colors from rust to red
I watch the beautiful colors drift
To the ground when birds are being fed

The bluejays are handsome in the golden leaves
I will close my eyes and picture these
On days when I feel blue jay blue
I will close my eyes and think of you

You are handsome and mischievous like bluejays
I am missing you and your clever ways
It is time to stop by for a treat
The one I have for you is sweet

Stop by soon and change my blue
Stop by with love
I am missing you

Take Time

He stands a beacon of integrity
His masculinity beams with light
Her heart is full of love for him
They love the love they share at night
Sometimes they share it in the day
Some afternoons and some mornings
You should never just walk in
Without the proper warnings

These two share a love so rare
They nurture it and give it care
Hugs and kisses start love making
They do not mind when time needs taking
Sometimes love can be so strong
Taking time is never wrong
When they take time for love it is right
Be it morning, afternoon, or night

Fate

How is it love finds you?
When you were not looking
When you did not want feelings to feel
How does love plant itself?
And is this love real?

When you stay on God's path
Following His calling
You find yourself falling in love
And still falling
You just keep falling in love even deeper
How does that happen when God is your keeper

How did love find me?
When my heart was hiding
Love found my heart and is living and abiding
I asked myself if this love was right
Or did it come too late
God reassured me I can love again
This new love, it was fate

Meditating

I meditate to still my wanted dreams
Timing is not ours
It seems
My mind goes crazy over you
Sheer craziness
Till my soul said no
Be still dear mind
This is not your show
Be still dear mind and let your thoughts be few
When it comes to love
The soul knows what to do

I closed my eyes
Golden trajectories fell like rain
A portal opened to the sky
The sky of my mind above the soul
Blissfully, the soul emerged
Relinquishing the mind of its control
How wonderful to listen to the soul
To hear nothing in a place
Where nothing is everything

Fate and timing are divine
In God's timing
He will give me what is mine
To help my mind, I will meditate
To help the craziness
While I wait for fate

Heart Shadows

He wore her shadow on his heart
Visions of her filled his mind
He spoke to her, and his voice softened
He would wink at her
That turned her on he would find
She had feelings also stirring
Visions of him re-occurring
She wore his shadow on her heart
He was handsome, strong, and smart
She smiled at him at every glance
She touched his arms, every chance
She found
Love's shadows live on hearts as well
As shadows cast on ground

Boomerang

She lived many years living her faith
Songs of faith she soothingly sang
She began to feel what she did not want to feel
She dismissed it but it was a boomerang

The more she threw it back to life
The more it returned with greater force
She never expected love to find her
Now love had to take its course

She tried to throw off the emotional turmoil
But was tethered to what destiny had planned
Now it was a full-blown love awakening
The boomerang finds you...
When it comes from God's hand

Planting Flirts

I sowed my seeds of love in his heart
With heartfelt flirting
For love to start
My words of love were not teasing for fun
I wanted to be his only one
I planted chosen words
Though not to deep
I wanted them to surface
When he cannot sleep
At night when sleep is hard to find
I wanted to be there in his mind
I spoke my flirty offerings
Chosen words to let love grow
If I did a decent job of planting
His love for me will start to show

The Whisper

I felt his breath in his whisper in my ear
I put my hands on his arm
And he pulled me near
Then I looked at his face into his eyes
He winked at me, another surprise
He drove me home and as we held hands
Love was calling
Sometimes it commands
Tonight was our night
To follow love's demands
Whispered words and locking eyes
Warm hands and touching thighs
Making love as time lays still
It started with a whispered thrill
I love my man, he is all man
No man can whisper like he can
No other woman will feel his breath
Whisper in their ear
His breath is mine
And only mine to hear

Love Spoke to the Wall

I spoke to the wall and the wall talked back
Saying nothing, though I understood
He was stonewalling my love
He could not accept it though knew he should
Love can permeate the strongest walls
When love is destined and becomes awake
Take those walls down and build a bed
We have so much love to make

I know all about your stone wall
I was stubborn and mine was tall
God worked on mine, it started inside
Love grew strong and could not hide
I was not looking when love found me
It broke me down so painfully
Then it grew to a radiant light
It made me want you every night

Your wall is not immune to love
My wall fell and I fell too
Love is stronger than stone walls
It is time for me to be with you
I speak my words of love to your wall
It is time to go, it is time to fall
Love now wants us heart to heart
With no walls keeping us apart

Missing My Ram

Her longing for him was deep
She often saw him in her sleep
She loved those dreams when she felt his touch
In that dimension love was real
And meant so much

His missed caress, his arms that held her
Love would stir an endless longing
He was absent from their once belonging

She patiently waits to see his face
She waits to melt in his embrace
It is his face that brings her peace
When he holds her and is slow to release

Being separated can make love stronger
Tonight, she will not have to wait
Any longer

Eye Conversation

My heart stores these memories
Those eye conversations with my man
The way he sees me in eye conversation
It moves me, it really can
We will be enjoying the company
When we are together with friends
I look forward to leaving together
When the gathering ends
All throughout the evening
We find ourselves looking at each other
With heartfelt glances or stares
Then he winks at me, and he looks serious
Then my passion flares
When we walk out the door, I reach for his hand
I feel it in my body
He has something planned
Those glances with eyes glazed
The passions that were raised
I foresee us ending the evening
With both of us
Feeling amazed

Love Finds You

He was not looking for love
It found him and it made a place
His mind was eased when she was near
He was happy to see her face
He felt her love
That made him strong
She loved him unconditionally
Every day, all day long
He was overwhelmed with love
There were times he hid a tear
He is a better man today
Now that he has her here

She was not looking for love
It came to her, she was off guard
She met him and deep feelings grew
She fell for him hard
He was hers and hers alone
She felt safe when by his side
Occasionally, she would cry
The love she felt, she could not hide
God's ways cannot be understood
Mysteries not to be known
God made plans and crossed their paths
He was hers, and now
She his own

Afternoon Nap?

You wanted me to lay for a Sunday nap
You want to cuddle before you sleep
Believe me, every cuddle you give me
Is in my memory to keep

Those memories stay in my heart
With your heartfelt words to never part
This afternoon you did not fall asleep
We gave into love
When it grew deep
We can get our sleep at night
This afternoon you held me tight
Our cuddling and kissing
Gave into dismissing a nap

I am happy, handsome, that you were not tired
Today it was not a nap I desired
Any day that ends in Y
I am willing to pass on a nap
(Oh my)

Everyday Days

There are ordinary days
Simple everyday days for everyone
Even me
Even on such ordinary days
It is you I will see
Be it in my presence, my thoughts
Or my heart
Your extraordinary love
Will most certainly never part
The feeling of your love
Is not slight enough to ignore
Even on those everyday days
When we are home and close the door
And when we are home to stay
I want to give you my love
Every day... every day
In my own extraordinary way
To live extraordinarily in love
With my handsome lover
Nothing ordinary here
When we are under the cover

A Ring

If he should offer me a ring
Diamonds would not be my thing
I would want to wear the same band that he wears
I do not need a diamond that glares
I would love to wear a band that he chooses
To remind me of him and that he chose me
Diamonds and jewels can be worn by others
A band that matches his is all I want to see

Are You Coming?

When he walked me to the door
He kissed me and I wanted more
I wanted more; I wanted it all
But I was a lady, I will wait for his call

The next date we were holding hands
He spoke words that went to my heart
I could not wait till he took me home
For the kiss at the door and what might start

The way he kissed me, the passion was deep
His arms were holding me so tight
My hands were holding the sides of his face
I thought I would faint, my head felt light

He kissed me good at my front door
He kissed me and I wanted more
But I was a lady and after all
He held me so I would not fall

He is my man, and I cannot wait
To be with him on another date
The next time we get to my door
He is coming in to give me more

He is coming in and he is going to stay
I will be a lady in my own way
The lady in me will be a woman that night
And I will be loving my man all right

He is coming in and we will lock the door
Next time we will both be wanting more

Wake Up Kiss

He was sleeping and I slipped in to lay on him
Admiring his face
He opened his eyes and smiled with love
He gave me a soft embrace
We kissed and our lips locked
His lower lip between my lips
His hands slid down lower on my body
I felt his hands brushing my hips
We kissed a little more and
In a firm voice he said "I love you"
I let him go back to sleep
After I said "I love you too"

My Smart Man

I marvel at his intelligence
Everything he says makes sense
He tells me I am beautiful
And likes it that I am no nonsense
When he tells me he loves my body
When he tells me that he loves my mind
When he says our love making is wonderful
And that I am one of a kind
When he tells me I am a terrific cook
And some recipes should be in a book
When he tells me I look sexy in lace
He lets me know by the look on his face
When he tells me I do not look my age
I should have put this one on the top of the page
How did I ever get a man who is this smart
A man who is also handsome, loving, and strong
I will believe anything he has to say
Every day and all day long

Stop For a Hug

I was going to pass behind him
To go where I was going
His arm reached back to stop me
And me not knowing
He wanted to stop me, and he did

That arm pulled me to his chest
Where his other arm joined to hold me
He embraced me with his love
That he never hid

His hugs and embracing
Feel as if heaven holds me
When you can feel love emanating
From the strength of his embrace

I like to pause for a moment
Every time I feel this
And look up to my man
To see the love on his face

Silence Speaks Volumes

His masculinity silences my words
My chest expands and my breath slows
My intuition tells me it is time for love
He requests of me to remove my clothes

Lover, there is no other man like you
You are the only one to move me this way
Everything in this life that I have, I will give
To you, today and all day, every day
My love for you is at a mystical level
I silence my words now and my eyes glaze
Do to me lover what we need to do
As my eyes stay focused on your gaze

I love you handsome and your masculine way
I will be everything you need in every way
The love between us will never be broken
I silenced my words, but my body has spoken

Space for Love

As much as I love to see his face
I will make sure he has his space
I am not a clingy or needy one
Unless it is time for bedroom fun
I give my man his manly hours
To himself or to what suits his needs
I do not mind mowing the lawn
Doing gardening or pulling weeds
He can catch up on his phone
Or take a nap when he is alone
Or visit friends or watch his sports
I am blessed that I am the one he courts
I will go the extra mile
To give him space, to see him smile
No nagging woman will I ever be
To change the way
Oh my, the way he loves me

Lightning Brought Thunder

I suppressed my love
For so many years it lay hidden
The thought of a man loving me
Was all but forbidden
My clouds remained dark
Building for a storm
Waiting for love to fall as rain
As in the summer, when it falls warm
When you have dark clouds above you
And you anticipate rain
Only it never starts falling
It brings a drought of love pain
I prayed to God for a lightning strike
He sent me thunder
In the form of a man, I would like
Lord, I more than like him
I love my man of thunder
He removed all my dark clouds
He vanished them asunder
I was ready to catch the lightning
My heart was ready for a strike
Thank you, Lord, for sending me thunder
He has a powerful love that I like

Closed for the Season

The ram is at rest
He travels at his own choosing
Avoiding his she
His interest he was losing
Though he never forgets
The scent that will draw him back
Now is not the season
She will find company with the pack
The ram and she
Have an inner understanding
When it is time for their season
She looks forward to his commanding

Slow Clock

Time moves slow when you are not here
Missing you one day feels like one year
Come home to me soon
I want to see you more
I miss you and love you
Please walk through my door
Loneliness plagues me
I am here feeling vexed
I miss your strong arms
(At least send a text)

He Has My Back

I love my man, he has my back
He is always there for me
He pats my back when he is proud
I can turn around and see
He is there
He has my back and
I am not going anywhere

When I lean back, and he is there
He will pull himself closer to me
I love it when he holds me this way
I look back
He is there
He has my back and
He is not going anywhere

The love he gives takes fear away
Loneliness will not see the light of day
He has my back and my heart, and all of me
I am grateful he is there
Grateful with me, he will always be

Thoughtful and Thankful

I love it when he thinks of me
He will say "come home, I will grill you a steak"
Of course, I will be there ASAP
When there is food, he wants to make
You see,
He cares for me to see I am fed
My appreciation will show later
In our bed
But first I will clear the table of dishes
He can settle his food as he manifests his wishes
He knows I will thank him for caring for my needs
Lucky for him
I am the one that he feeds

Fate and Destiny

My wait was long
But my reward was great
As destiny held hands with fate
Patience all but bled me dry
Time only crawled, it did not fly
Then love persevered
And when it did arrive
It breathed for me
It was alive
The lonely past is now erased
Love gave me amnesia from all I faced
His love consumed my mind and heart
Comfort, destiny did impart
We belong to each other
Our gift from fate
Love this deep was worth the wait

The Color of Love

If love could be a color
Ours would be gold
Gold as the sun
Rising and spilling on the horizon
Gold as the sun glimmering
Through the tops of the trees
Majestic golden gold
As the sun is ready to set
As gold as the streets in heaven
Though not yet
Let us live in the gold of our love
For the remainder of our years
Sharing our love and company
With family and friends
And some cold golden beers
Our love for each other we will treasure
And hold
If love could be a color
Our color would be gold

Quiet Days

We will have quiet days
No need to speak for the sake of speaking
Some days the quiet
Is all we are seeking
Those quiet days
I may glance at him once in a while
And if he looks back
I will smile
He will smile too and then
I will be the one to wink
He will ask "what are you thinking about?"
I will reply "what do you think?"

I do love the quiet days
When we make love in a quiet haze
Just soft slow words and soft slow ways
That is what happens on quiet days

That is what we do on our quiet days

Our Love

There will be no hurt between us
Our love will cover all
We will be considerate of each other's feelings
We love each other and after all
Compared to our love
Troubles will be small

We love each other
That is what we do
We make love, we embrace and kiss
Troubles will be nothing
Compared to this
Making love with each other
Embracing and kissing
Troubles and hurt
Will be the only things missing

No troubles or hurt will cause us to fall
The way we love each other
Our love will cover all

End of Days

When we are old and wearing gray
I think we will still want to play
I will never stop making love with you
Even if those times are few
I will love you to my dying day
Or yours
When one of our flames go away
We will say good-bye
Only bye for now
Twin flames will join again
Some day
Some how

When One of Us Leaves

When one of us leaves
Let me be the first to go
He can stay, he is stronger
We had the greatest love you could ever know

He will still enjoy hunting and fishing
He will have a dog and drink some beers
If he was the one to leave me first
I would be the one crying my tears
Though I would be eternally grateful
That I was the one to have the love of this man
And if I do go first
And he wants to shed a tear or two
When he says good-bye to me, for now
He can

Forever On My Heart

I am not one for wearing tattoos
Though I would wear one with your name
A heart that bares a set of ram horns
With your name crossing over a flame
I love you ram
I love you, my ram
My greatest love
With you I will share
I will wear your name
Across my heart
Forever more, you will be there

Dream Love

Is my glorious ram only my imagination?
Or is he alive, breathing, and real?
I created my handsome ram lover
To live in my mind, he is mine to feel
He is in my heart, my soul, and my mind
I am waiting here dear ram
For you to find
I will surely know you when you come my way
When you finally manifest
I know you will stay
My love is waiting, and I am saving it all for you
It is amazing what manifesting
And an imagination can do
With your deepest faith and believing
Your deepest dreams can come true
I am waiting for you, ram
Dear Ram, I love you
When you are finally mine
I may get that tattoo

THE END

A "heart" felt thank you to the artist Robbie Jelsma from Springfield South Dakota for the beautiful artwork on the cover. He captured my mind.